# The High Coast

## a world heritage site

LÄNSSTYRELSEN VÄSTERNORRLANDS LÄN

NATUR VÅRDS VERKET

**This book can be ordered from**
**Skule Naturum, Skuleberget, S-870 33 Docksta**
**Tel: +46-613-40171, fax: +46-613-40424**
**E-mail: skulenaturum@y.lst.se**

**ISBN   91-974680-0-2**

Project manager: **Mats Henriksson, Arne Eriksson**
Editor: **Lars-G Candell**
Copy editor: **Gustaf Forssell**
Design: **Anita Forssell**
Production: **Flygande Huset**

Authors: **Margareta Bergvall** - Humans and the Sea
**Lars-G Candell -** The Road to the High Coast, Places to Discover
**Erika Ingvald** - Bedrock, the Glacial Ice Sheet, and the Sea
**Jan W Mascher** - The Flora and the Rising Land, Animal Life Along the High Coast, Protected Areas
**Märit Nilsson** - Roaming through a Wondrous Landscape, Bedrock, the Glacial Ice Sheet and the Sea, The
World Heritage Convention, Rising Land or Falling Seas, The Landscape Continually Challenges Me

Translation: **Accent Language Service (www.accent-sweden.com)**

Expert advice: **Margareta Bergvall** The County Museum of Västernorrland,
**Leif Grundberg** County Administrative Board, **Erika Ingvald** scientific journalist,
**Rolf Löfgren** The National Swedish Environment Protection Board,
**Jan W Mascher** Botanist, **Christer Nordlund** Umeå University,
**Maria Olsson** County Administrative Board

Printing: **Prinfo Accidenstryckeriet Sundsvall 2003**
The first Swedish edition published in 2002
Text type face: Times New Roman 10p
Heading type face: Myriad Roman
Paper: Gotic Silk 170 g

*Front cover: Black dolerite seam cuts through beautiful red rapakivi granite. The High Coast with Skuleberget Mountain to the right. Photo: Kjell Ljungström*

*Inside front cover: Sand with a layer of pulverised shells, primarily from sea mussels, and the Calypso Orchid.*
*Photo: Jan W Mascher and Lennart Vessberg*
*Small till-capped hill west of Slåttdalsberget in Skuleskogen National Park.*
*Photo: Kjell Ljungström*

*Back cover: Shingles along a shore of the High Coast. Photo: Kjell Ljungström*

*Back inside cover: Shingle beach with Högbonden Island in the background. Different types of granites and dolerite. Photo: Lennart Vessberg*
*Rotsidan's dolerite rock slab shoreline. Photo: Lars-G Candell*
*Rotsidan. Poem: Gunnar Fredriksson*

# Preface

The High Coast is in the County of Västernorrland, right in the centre of Sweden, right in the middle of Scandinavia. The High Coast's precipitous and varied landscape has fascinated visitors throughout the ages. The steep cliffs, rolling hills and narrow valleys accent the placid lakes and deep bays along the coast. People have always been drawn here to experience the unusual beauty of the countryside, the fishing and the sea. Tourism has become a part of everyday life in the region.

When The High Coast was added to UNESCO´s World Heritage List in November 2000, it was due to the area's unique geology, a geology that gives the region its renowned beauty. The High Coast is one of those fascinating places on earth where isostatic land uplift is still going on, long after the glacial ice sheet has melted. Isostatic land uplift is the upward return movement of the Earth's crust following glaciation, when the crust was depressed by the weight of the ice. This is readily observable but the area's uniqueness lies in the extent of the land uplift, 286 metres above sea level, the greatest in the world. The region is a prime area for research into isostatic land uplift, a phenomenon that was first demonstrated and studied here.

The High Coast is also home to the highest coastline in the world on Skuleberget Mountain, a spectacular 286 metres down to the sea. The bedrock, the glacial ice sheet and the sea have dramatically shaped the landscape and created unique sights, such as till-caped hills, shingle fields, and onion-shaped caves, all in close geographic proximity.

The honour of being named as a World Heritage Site fills the residents of the region and nature lovers with pride. We hope that the views, waterscapes and forests will encourage visitors travelling the E4 to make a detour to experience this dramatic rising landscape, the exciting flora with species from different climatic periods, and the remnants of earlier cultures. We hope that all those who enjoy the outdoors, artists, musicians, and researchers will visit and maybe stay in the High Coast to enrich both themselves and our common world heritage.

All this spurs us on to make the High Coast an even more attractive destination. Welcome to the High Coast - a World Heritage Site.

Härnösand and Stockholm, May 2002

Gerhard Larsson
County Governor of Västernorrland

Lars-Erik Liljelund
Director-General
Swedish Environmental Protection Agency

# Contents

**Chronology**

There are several methods for dating the geological and historical events that took place over the last 20,000 years. Due to differing resolution, the results from these methods may differ, in some cases with as much as thousands of years. In this book we use varve chronology when discussing the age of events that are related to the latest ice-age. This method is based on counting varves of sediments in the same way as one may count annual rings in a tree, so called dendrocrhronology. The deposits from the melting ice became layered due to the difference in sedimentary transport between summer and winter. Carbon-14 is used for the section covering archaeology.

# Roaming through a wondrous landscape

*Slåttdalsberget in Skuleskogen National Park with Slåttdalsskrevan Crevice at the centre of the picture. Tärnättvattnen Lakes and Näskefjärden Bay can be seen in the background.*

The wonders of nature have always fascinated people. If we haven't understood something, we've created myths and tales to explain it. With its steep face to the east and its dark spruce forest to the north-west, Skuleberget Mountain captures our attention. This mountain and forest have both frightened and attracted generations of people. People still recount stories and myths of the bandits that roamed the area, and an old execution site by a nearby lake serves as a reminder of the past.

Today hikers, skiers, and climbers aren't so easily scared by stories of bandits. They are more interested in hills with steep faces and rock walls. Visitors can now easily reach the summit of Skuleberget Mountain using the chair lift. From here, they can see a vast countryside, seemingly unchanged by time, but which is in fact changing constantly, at an imperceptible rate. The High Coast rises eight millimetres a year and will continue to rise for at least several thousand years.

*Bare rock washed clean by the waves, shingle fields, Tärnättholmarna.*

*Rövargrottan (Robber's Cave) was renamed Kungsgrottan (King's Cave) for King Karl XI.*

*The peak of Skuleberget Mountain rose above the cold Yoldia Sea 9600 years ago.*

## At the top of Skuleberget Mountain

The spruce forest at the top is thick and the undergrowth is lush, but on the edge, the rocks are bare. This is part of the reason that the High Coast became a World Heritage Site in 2000.

The waves of the cold Yoldia Sea washed the rocks clean of soil 9600 years ago. At that time, the top of Skuleberget Mountain barely rose above the deep, blue sea to form an island. The waves couldn't reach the top of the peak, so the till left behind by the ice sheet remained. This is where the spruce trees laid their roots. For centuries, the land rose higher and higher out of the sea. The bare rocks tell where the first shore lay, known as the highest coastline, currently at 286 metres above sea level.

The landscape seems limitless. Hills and forests stretch out as far as the eye can see. Lakes glisten and marshes glow yellow in the low points between the hills.

European Highway 4 (E4) meanders below. But few of the modern drivers think about the wayfarer's of the past and the fortune seekers from Nolaskog Forest, north of the Skule Forest. In the winter, they headed south to sell flax they had grown on the fertile fields and skins they had traded for with the Sami and other hunters from the inland regions. In those days, they wanted to travel quickly through Skuleskogen Forest to reach the taverns in Spjute and Docksta.

Before the road was known as E4, it was called Highway 13. Even before there were highways, it was known as Norrstigen Trail. After the Swedish king, Karl XI (1672-1697), passed by here on an inspection of his kingdom, the Robber's Cave on Skuleberget Mountain was renamed King's Cave. It is said though that the king did not actually dare to visit the cave. Parts of Norrstigen Trail can still be seen today.

From the top, visitors can see how the narrow stretches of flat land were effectively used for farming. These fields were once bays in the sea that lay between the hills. As the land rose, the bays dried out and became fertile farm land.

For the best view, visitors should walk down the mountain trail. Once down, the trail darts into a beautiful forest coloured by a variety of flowers and plants. In the spring, Liverleafs, Wood Anemones, and Lilies of the Valley accompany hikers in the High Coast's forests. Early in the spring, hikers make their way through carpets of Liverleafs.

## The reddish granite

The High Coast has many colours. Visitors see light blue when they hike out of the forest and see the hills and the sky open before them. The rapakivi granite provides a red hue to the landscape. At sunset, the High Coast glistens like gold, bringing the shingle fields to life. The sunlight highlights shades of gray and the lichen covered red rocks that turn dark green when it rains.

Rapakivi, a Finnish word, means rotten rock. Rapakivi falls apart into square blocks, perfect for serving as stepping stones for hikers along the High Coast Hiking Trail through Slåttdalsskrevan Crevice in Skuleskogen Forest. The red granite crumbles into rough gravel under boots. Nordingrå Granite, the provincial stone of Ångermanland, is also a type of rapakivi.

The winter frost leaves its mark on the hill and boulders. The forces of nature seem to balance each other out. As the land rises from the sea after being pressed down by the weight of the ice, the wind, water and frost break the rising land apart from above.

In the past, a visitor could hear the people from Käl harvesting hay for their animals on Slåttdalsmyran. While they harvested the hay by hand, their horses would graze freely in the forest. As you approach Slåttdalsskrevan Crevice today, the only sound you hear is your own heartbeat.

## From mussel shells to orchids

The eroding hills along the High Coast fertilize the coastal vegetation. Villmyran in Norrfällsviken and Halsviksravinen Ravine on Räfsön are perfect for flower enthusiasts. They have an abundance of orchids, such as Calypso Orchids, Ghost Orchids, Bird's-nest Orchids, One-leaved Bog-orchids, and Narrow-leaved Marsh-orchids.

Keep your eyes on the road cuts and sand pits. A violet streak in the sand can be the remains of shells from mussels and snails that lived in ancient seas. Earlier incarnations of the Baltic had a higher salt content than today's sea. The shells were covered by sand, and the rising land moved them far from the present shoreline. Just think about holding mussel shells that are thousands of years old and that are so white that it looks like they were deposited yesterday. Now they supply calsium to orchids and other flowers. As you walk along the shoreline, it is easy to pass the Northern Rock-cress without noticing it, but it is also a rarity. The Northern Rock-cress

*The climbing trail on Skuleberget Mountain. Nowaday people are not afraid of the Skule robbers.*

*Slåttdalsskrevan Crevice in Skuleskogen Forest.*

originates from the Norwegian Atlantic coast and prefers rocky soil near the sea such as along the Rotsidan shoreline. The High Coast is the only place where it grows along the entire Baltic coast. Hazel and Norway Maple trees prefer southern slopes such as on Omneberget. Other slopes are the home of such alpine rarities as Purple Saxifrage.

## Using nature as your map

Archaeologists use the rising land to map the past. Signs from earlier periods of human history can be found at different levels above the sea, such as the grave cairns left behind by the mysterious people of the Bronze Age. Along the shore they built cairns of stone for their dead. At the Näske summer farm in Skuleskogen Foerest, one of their ancient cemeteries established during the early Bronze Age (1000-600 BC) is now 40 metres above its original seashore location.

Archaeologists look for traces of people in areas that once were sheltered coast. Early humans seem to have built their settlements where they had access to food, fresh water, and shelter. The sea provided fish and seals, streams provided water, and forests provided wood. It was safer to have a view of the entrance into the bay, which protected them from storms and enemies. Transportation was mainly done using boats.

When the land rose so much that the settlements were too far from water, the people moved down to the shoreline again. Abandoned settlements have moved further and further up the slopes. The same holds true for more modern fishing villages such as Gammhamnen on the island of Storön and Sandviken on Ulvön Island.

## The landscape changes

You would think that the landscape is firmly anchored in the bedrock. At least this is how it feels when standing on the rock slabs by Skeppsmalen or Berghamn or when slowly making your way on Norrfällsviken's shingle fields, which take up nearly the entire point.

But the landscape is changeing. As the land arises from the water, rocks are rolled by the waves and broken apart by the coastal ice. When rocks are beyond the waves, lichen gains a foothold and erodes and weathers the rocks. The grooves on rock slabs reveal the passage of the ice that melted 9600 years ago. Eventually, the ice sheet will return, but no one knows.

*At the left*
*The peak of Slåttdalsberget and the archipelago off the coast of Skuleskogen National Park in the distance.*

*Many answers can be found by studying the World Heritage Site, but new questions always arise.*

# Bedrock, the glacial ice sheet and the sea

The today's landscape of the High Coast is largely the result of the most recent Ice Age and the consequent uplifting of the land. The steep cliffs and exiting topography are the consequence of geologic processes that created the rocks between 1200 and 2000 million years ago. The oldest remaining bedrock in the area, known as greywacke, is a mixture of sand and clay deposited in the sea.

Approximately 1800 to 1900 million years ago, these greywackes were depressed into the earth's crust as mountains were formed. The rocks were converted by heat, pressure and folding. The process placed orignally horizontal layers in a vertical direction. At the same time magma intruded into the greywackes and solidified into such rocks as primary granite and younger Härnö granite.

## Gabbro, anorthosite and red rapakivi granite

Most of the High Coast bedrock consists of the darker gabbro, the lighter anorthosite, and the red rapakivi granite. The Finnish word rapakivi means rotten stone and refers to the fact that this type of rock tends to break apart and crumble to gravel. Rapakivi and similar rocks were formed between 1500 and 1600 million years ago. Today, researchers believe that rapakivi granite originates from melted older granite in the lower part of the earth's crust. Gabbro and anorthosite originate from melted granite in the deeper mantle. According to one interpretation, the melted rock intruded into shear zones that reached as deep as the earth's mantle. The shear zones were formed when the old mountain chain collapsed from the force of gravity.

## Sandstones and dolerite dykes

Between 1200 and 1500 million years ago, the upper rock layers were eroded. The weathered material was deposited in river deltas and transformed into coarse-grained, reddish and grey Jotnian sandstone with layers of dark violet clay slate. The remains of this sandstone are found on land at thicknesses of up to 65 metres, thanks to the fact that they were protected from erosion by a resistant layer of dolerite. The sandstone that once lay upon the dolerite has eroded on land, but in the Gulf of Bothnia, it has thicknesses on average of 1000 metres.

The layer of dolerite, which is between 250 and 300 metres thick, was formed about 1200 million years ago. Movements in the inner parts of the earth caused faulting. Parts of the bedrock were lifted while other parts sank. There are dolerite dykes throughout the entire area from when basaltic magma from the earth's mantle intruded into the fault zones and between layers of sandstone.

*At the left*
*Onion-shaped cave on northern Ulvön Island. The rock cracked, allowing boulders to break loss from the rock wall. The movement of the waves turned the boulders into a grinder which cut out a cave.*

Nordingrå granite is the local name for rapakivi granite, which is found along the High Coast.

*The bird cliff on Skrubban Island.*
*Even though dolerite is so evident and often very dramatic to see, especially on islands, it is actually only a small part of the geologic history of the area compared to rapakivi, gabbro and anorthosite.*

*Previous pages*
*Dolerite rock surface smoothed by waves and a shingle field in the background with a clearly defined shoreline bank on Trysunda Island.*

*Sweden was completely covered by the glacial ice sheet during the last ice age, known as the Weichsel Ice Age. It may have looked something like this when the hilltops emerged from the melting ice. This picture is from modern-day Greenland.*

*This is how it might have looked 9600 years ago when the glacial ice sheet melted away from the High Coast. This picture is from modern-day Greenland.*

The glacial ice sheet was 3000 metres thick above the High Coast. Skuleberget Mountain's peak is 295 metres above the sea and the height of the High Coast Bridge's pylons is 188 metres.

## High hills sloping straight into the sea

It might have been at this point, 1200 to 1500 million years ago, that the High Coast became a coastline. In what is now south-east Sweden, the bedrock was eroded to a flat surface, the Subcambrian peneplain. South of the High Coast, this level land surface swings into the Gulf of Bothnia and does not reappear on land again until north of the High Coast. The area that makes up the World Heritage Site was not affected by this process, and the High Coast became the only area around the Baltic Sea where high hills slope into the sea.

The High Coast's dramatic landscape with deep bays and high hills was formed long after the formation of the rocks they are made of, when running water and the glacial ice sheet wore down and removed broken rocks along major cracks and faults.

## Glacial ice sheet

Over a period of millions of years, on several occasions the earth cooled so much that large glacial ice masses spread across the northern and southern hemispheres in areas that today are free from ice.

Variations in the heating from the sun and changes to the earth's orbit are often cited as causes of climate changes. In addition, the processes that very slowly move continents across the earth's surface also play a role. Periods of many and large volcanic eruptions contribute to change the concentration of greenhouse gases in the atmosphere. Since the beginning of the industrial era, it is also possible that changes in the atmosphere are increasingly the result of human activities.

The oldest known ice age was 2300 million years ago. Five large ice ages have occurred over the last 800 million years. Between these relatively short cold periods, the climate has been considerably warmer.

Forty million years ago, the previously mild climate began to cool. This process intensified 10 to 15 million years ago. The average temperature fell and an era with drastic shifts between cold and warm periods began. This pattern increased 2.5 million years ago. Cold periods - ice ages - alternated with warmer periods with climates similar to today's climate.

Researchers do not know much about the periods of glaciation in Scandinavia before the most recent one, known as the Weichsel glaciation, since it practically erased all traces of previous glaciations.

Glacial ice sheets expand slowly and melt quickly. Cool summers and mild winters with excessive precipitation cause glaciers to grow, forming glacial ice sheets. The snow does not melt during the summer and more snow is added from year to year. As the snow cover expands, the weight of the snow forms ice.

During the last period of glaciation in Europe, the glaciers in Scandinavia's mountain chain grew during cold periods and eventually spread out and formed glacial ice sheets.

## The most recent glacial ice sheet

The Weichsel glaciation began 115,000 years ago. It was interrupted a couple of times with somewhat milder periods and then went into its main phase about 70,000 years ago. The largest ice coverage occurred 20,000 years ago. From its centre point in Scandinavia, the ice sheet covered northern Germany and western Russia. It was thickest, about 3000 metres, over today's High Coast. The immense weight of the ice sheet depressed the earth's crust along the High Coast more than 800 metres from its pre-glacial level. During the same period, large parts of North America and the southern hemisphere were also covered by glacial ice sheets.

## The land rebounds

The ice margin was along the High Coast 9600 years ago. About 800 years later, nearly the entire glacial ice sheet had melted away. About 18,000 years ago, major climate warming began, causing the glacial ice sheet to begin retreating. As the ice became thinner, its weight lessened, allowing the earth's crust to begin rebounding. In the beginning, the rate of rebound was rapid at more than 10 centimetres a year. It then slowed. The velocity rate of land uplift decreased.

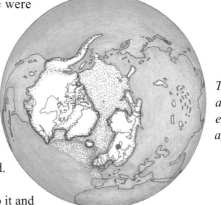

*The glacial ice sheets and sea ice's maximum extent 20,000 years ago.*

Imagine a freshly baked bun. Press your thumb down into it and then release it. You can see how the surface of the bun rebounds to its original shape. When the ice melted and the pressure lessened, the earth's crust began to return to its original shape, just as a bun does. By the time the ice had melted away from the High Coast, the area had already risen 500 metres, a process that took 8400 years. Over the next 9600 years - up to the present day - the area rose an additional 286 metres. The earth rebounds 8 mm per year, and researchers believe it will take another 5000 years for the final 50 metres.

The fact that this land uplift is so well illustrated in a relatively small and distinctive area contributed to the appointment of the High Coast as a World Heritage Site. No other place on earth has such a large total land uplift as the High Coast.

*The maximum extent of the ice cover by the most recent glacial ice sheet 20,000 years ago. The greatest depression made by the weight of the ice, approximately 800 metres, was at today's High Coast.*

*The size of the ice sheet over the North Sea, the Northern Arctic Ocean, and Siberia is still being debated.*

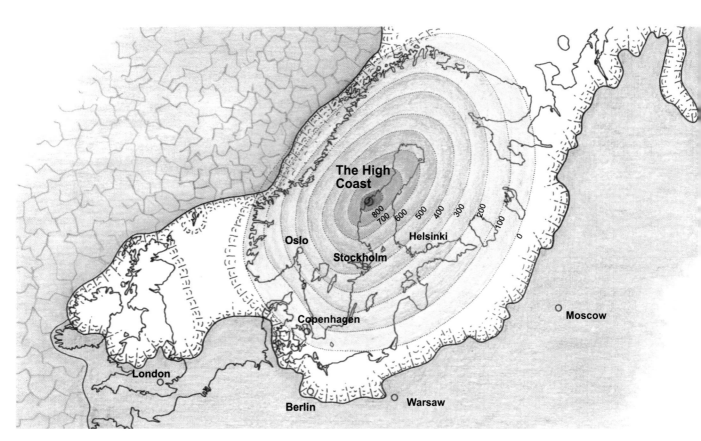

## The landscape from the Ice Age to the present and beyond

As the ice began to recede from the High Coast 9600 years ago, the land continued
unstoppable thrust upward out of the sea. The first small islets grew to islands. The isla…
grew and joined to create bays. Hills rose high above the water. The bays narrowed and w…
cut off making lakes. Small lakes began to fill in and turned into marshes. New islands r…
from the sea. And the process continues today. The sea works the till left behind by
the glacial ice sheet. The material is sorted into shingle, gravel and sand.

 People continue to change the landscape along side the forces of nature.
This has been true since the first fishermen along the shore and Stone
Age settlements on the sandy beaches appeared and to modern farms
on fertile sediment and fishing villages in sheltered bays.

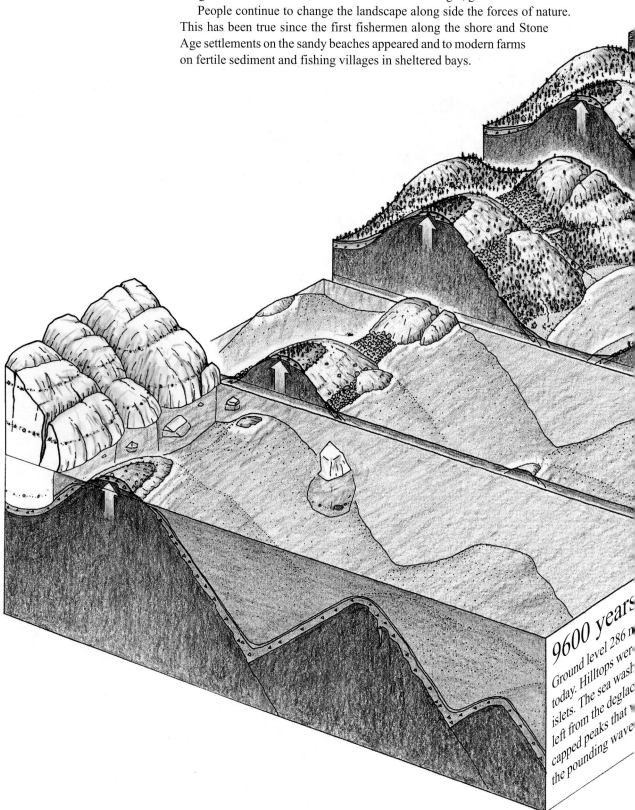

*9600 years*
*Ground level 286 m…*
*today. Hilltops wer…*
*islets. The sea wash…*
*left from the deglac…*
*capped peaks that …*
*the pounding wave…*

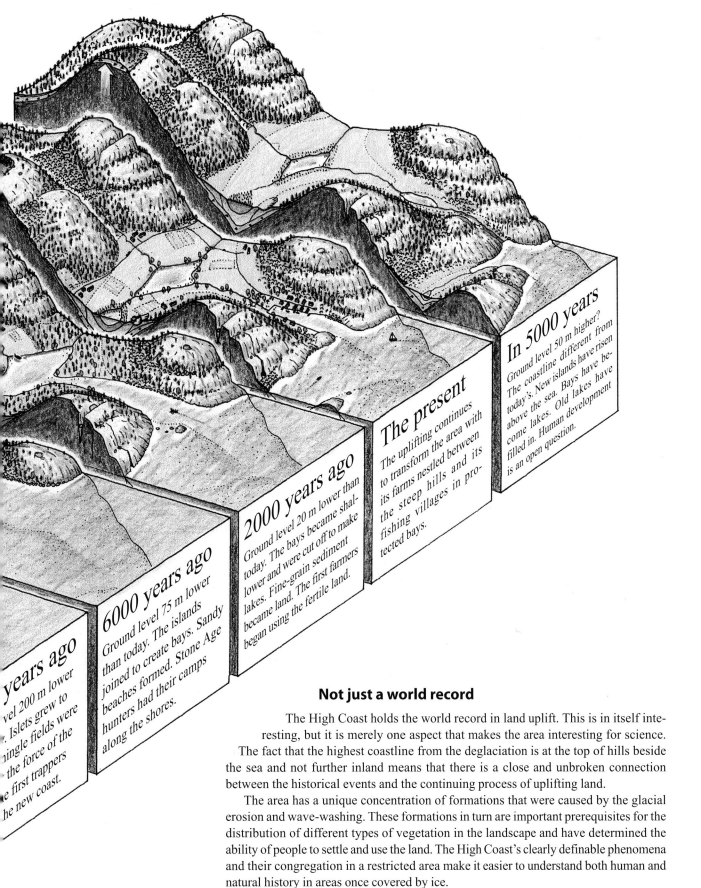

**... years ago**

... vel 200 m lower ... Islets grew to ...ingle fields were ... the force of the ...e first trappers ...he new coast.

**6000 years ago**

Ground level 75 m lower than today. The islands joined to create bays. Sandy beaches formed. Stone Age hunters had their camps along the shores.

**2000 years ago**

Ground level 20 m lower than today. The bays became shallower and were cut off to make lakes. Fine-grain sediment became land. The first farmers began using the fertile land.

**The present**

The uplifting continues to transform the area with its farms nestled between the steep hills and its fishing villages in protected bays.

**In 5000 years**

Ground level 50 m higher? The coastline different from today's. New islands have risen above the sea. Bays have become lakes. Old lakes have filled in. Human development is an open question.

## Not just a world record

The High Coast holds the world record in land uplift. This is in itself interesting, but it is merely one aspect that makes the area interesting for science. The fact that the highest coastline from the deglaciation is at the top of hills beside the sea and not further inland means that there is a close and unbroken connection between the historical events and the continuing process of uplifting land.

The area has a unique concentration of formations that were caused by the glacial erosion and wave-washing. These formations in turn are important prerequisites for the distribution of different types of vegetation in the landscape and have determined the ability of people to settle and use the land. The High Coast's clearly definable phenomena and their congregation in a restricted area make it easier to understand both human and natural history in areas once covered by ice.

*The smooth wave washed rock lifted from the sea by the rising land at Skags Point has a beautiful pattern of glacial striae. This is best seen from the lighthouse and on the rock face west of the chapel. A compass rose cut into the rock shows the direction of the striae and thus the movement of the ice.*

## The highest coastline

When the ice margin was along the High Coast, 9500-10000 years ago, today's Baltic Sea and the depressed land were covered by the cold Yoldia Sea.

The Yoldia Sea was filled with enormous amounts of runoff from the melting ice sheet. The Yoldia Sea was named after an Arctic Ocean mussel called *Yoldia arctica*. The name of the mussel was changed to *Portlandia arctica*, but the sea retained its name. The water flowed out into the Atlantic through a strait in northern Västergötland and kept brackish water from reaching the Baltic Sea. Only during a short period, when the Närke-strait became free of ice and before the land uplift made it shallow, brackish water was able to reach the Yoldia Sea. Bottom currents with brackish water never reached the Gulf of Bothnia.

Along the High Coast, only the highest hill tops rose above the water's surface creating small islands. Waves eroded deposits at the shoreline. The waves were very powerful since the sea was much larger than today's Gulf of Bothnia. Most of Finland was below sea level. The oldest shoreline with wave-washed surface is called the "highest coastline" and is clearly seen on Skuleberget Mountain, in Skuleskogen National Park and on Dalsberget hill.

The Yoldia Sea was followed by periods with varying degrees of fresh and brackish water in the Baltic Sea and Gulf of Bothnia. Ancylus Lake, 8000-9500 years ago, was characterised by fresh water and was named after the freshwater gastropod *Ancylus fluviatilis*.

About 8000 years ago, the Baltic Sea once again became characterised by brackish water which gradually spread north. This became possible thanks to the rising surface of the oceans as the glacial ice sheets melted away. By 5,000 years ago, the sea level had risen 35 metres. The uplift in land in southern Sweden was less than the rise in sea level, so ocean water was able to flow into the Baltic Sea. This phase of the Baltic Sea, known as the Litorina Sea - also named for a snail, after a gastropod, (*Littorina littorea*) - continues to this day.

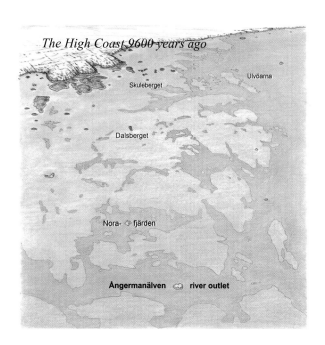

The High Coast 9600 years ago

Skuleberget

Ulvöarna

Dalsberget

Nora- fjärden

Ångermanälven river outlet

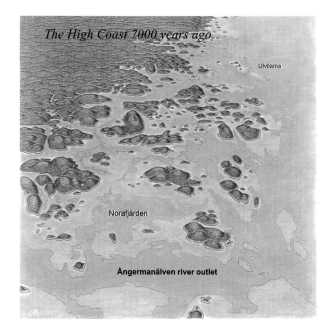

The High Coast 7000 years ago

Ulvöama

Norafjärden

Ångermanälven river outlet

From 8000 to 2500 years ago, the climate was somewhat warmer than today and the Litorina Sea had a higher salt content than today's Baltic Sea. This resulted in a flora and a fauna, which today are usually found at more southern latitudes with higher salt content.

The waves and currents transported shells and shell fragments from snails and mussels along the beaches. These shells fragments were embedded in layers of sand. The most common types of shell are from the common mussel, Mytilus edulis. These layers can be seen in sand pits and along road cuts, where they shimmer purple and white from the shells' mother-of-pearl. The shell fragments contain calsium, which benefits plants that thrive on calcium such as Early Marsh-orchids, Calypso Orchids and Ghost Orchids.

Today the Baltic Sea is the world's largest brackish water sea with flora and fauna from both fresh and brackish water. The Baltic Sea, the Bay of Bothnia and the Gulf of Bothnia will increasingly be characterised by fresh water over the coming 100 years because of the rising land and changes of the climate.

### In the path of the ice sheet

Glacial ice is plastic in nature and gravity moves glaciers downhill. Stones and blocks frozen in the underside of the ice erode and scar the bedrock, creating striae and other pressure marks. The grooves indicate in which direction the ice is moving.

When the ice melts, it leaves a landscape covered with till, a jumble of different types of rocks from microscopic to boulder size. Till covers three-fourths of Sweden's surface area.

### Till-capped hills

Till sits undisturbed on hilltops that today are above the highest coastline. These areas are overgrown with lush forests. Below these peaks, the waves of the Yoldia Sea washed away the topsoil leaving only the bare rock. These peaks are called till-capped hills. Skuleberget Mountain has the best-known till-capped hill and has become a symbol for the High Coast World Heritage Site.

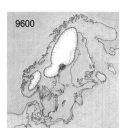

*Yoldia Sea*

*Ancylus Lake*

*Litorina Sea*

*Baltic Sea and Gulf of Bothnia*

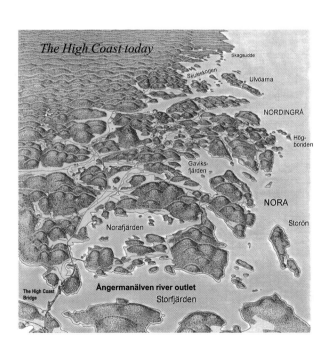

*The shingle field near the top of Högklin-*
*ten Hill. Down in Omnefjärden Bay, the*
*islands Skorporna and Örarna rise out of*
*the sea. In the background is Rävsön,*
*which has now become a peninsula.*

*The shingle field at Norrfällsviken.*
*Powerful storms and pressure from ice*
*have helped form the shingle fields and*
*created raised beaches.*

## From shingle fields to farm land

When the land began to rise, previously deposited sediments were exposed to the forces of waves and were moved around. The coarser particles, stones and gravel, remained close to the shore. The finer particles were washed out to sea where they slowly settled to the bottom and created clay and silt layers. This process has been ongoing for thousands of years and continues today. As the land rose, bays dried out and eventually could be used as farmland. Areas where coarser particles were deposited became forest lands.

Shingles are the coarsest sediment from wave-washed deposits. They consist of rounded stones and smaller boulders that have formed banks or fields. Shingle fields in the High Coast area are a distinctive feature of the landscape and are almost exclusively made up of rapakivi granite.

The world's highest shingle field with shore banks is on Högklinten Hill by Mjällom at 260 metres above the sea. The number of shingle fields and their occurrence at different levels all the way down to the current shoreline is a unique feature of the High Coast.

Severe storms and pressure from coastice have helped form the shingle fields and created raised beaches. A green-yellow lichen has established itself on the lee side of the banks, creating a bright band above the dull-grey of the shingle fields.

## Gigantic crevice

As the land rose, all areas below the highest coastline were exposed at some point to the waves and the forces of the coastice. Areas which were more easily eroded, such as in faults and cracks, could be washed clean by the sea. These carved out areas developed into crevices. One example of this is Slåttdalsskrevan Crevice in Skuleskogen National Park. This crevice in Rapakivi

granite is gigantic - forty metres deep, seven metres wide and two hundred metres long.

## Onion-shaped caves

Onion-shaped caves were formed by the combined forces of the waves, boulders and stones. They began with a crack in the rock along the shoreline. The rock cracked, allowing a boulder to break from the rock wall. The movement of the water turned the boulder into a grinder which cut out a cave. Some examples of this type of cave are on northern Ulvön Island, on Högbonden and at a height of 105 metres on Mjältön Island. Pot-holes are another example of stones and water erosion in the bedrock.

## Bays cut off to make lakes

As the land rises, bays become increasingly shallower. Narrow, shallow passages to the sea are cut off, creating fresh water lakes. Vågsfjärden Bay in Nordingrå still had contact with the sea 150 years ago. Today, it is a lake, the surface of which is about one metre above sea level. Even so, crustaceans that normally live in brackish water have been able to survive.

The narrow Trångsundet Strait can be seen from Stortorget Hill in Häggvik. The strait is only two metres deep and within 300 years, Häggvik's fishing village will be cut off from the sea.

Till is also called pinnmo in Swedish, from the word pina, meaning painful. This refers to the difficulty 19th century farmers had in growing crops on the till.

*Slåttdalsskrevan Crevice in Skuleskogen National Park.*

*Farmland in Nora with lakes formed from cut off bays.*

# The World Heritage Convention

*Dalsberget Hill is 333 metres above sea level and has a till-capped peak covered with evergreen forests. Houses in the village of Bergs by with Häggvik in the foreground.*

The World Heritage emblem symbolises the interdependence of culture and nature. The central square is a form created by people and the circle represents nature, the two being intimately linked. The emblem is round, like the world. At the same time, it is a symbol of protection.

On November 29, 2000 in Cairn, Australia, the World Heritage Committee added the High Coast as a World Heritage Site. The areas, places and buildings that receive World Heritage status are selected after careful review. World Heritage Sites are to have such an outstanding scientific and aesthetic value that their protection is of interest for all of humanity.

The idea behind the convention is that each World Heritage Site is an integral part of the world, and the present has a responsibility both for the past and the future. The World Heritage concept is a result of the growing global awareness of the environment and is a reaction to the consequences of the abuse of the earth's resources. The World Heritage Convention assumes that rich countries will help poorer countries to preserve their world heritage.

In 1972, the World Heritage Convention was approved by UNESCO, the UN's organ for education, science and culture, with headquarters in Paris. To date, 175 countries have signed the convention and have thereby committed to protecting the world's natural and cultural heritage. Sweden became a member in 1985.

As of the spring 2003, there are 730 World Heritage Sites, of which 563 are cultural world heritage sites, 144 are natural world heritage sites, and 23 are both cultural and heritage sites. One hundred twenty-five countries have sites.

## Geologic Congress to Skule

Högbom and De Geer had been rivals for some time. This rivalry though was put aside for a large international geologic congress in Stockholm in 1910. The dissolution of the union between Norway and Sweden had just occurred and Sweden had become smaller. The national elite felt this was the time to show off Sweden as a prominent country of science. Among the lectures, expeditions (including to Spitsbergen) and excursions was a trip to Skuleberget Mountain. The mountain thus became known outside of the Swedish geology community and since then the area has had a regular stream of researchers interested in land uplifting.

With the loss of Finland in 1809, Sweden had become much smaller. One way of regaining national pride was to point to Sweden's special geologic history and that nature was ensuring Sweden's growth. Both English amd Austrian geologists had explained their own countries' empires by pointing to their geology and Swedish geologists attempted similar arguments.

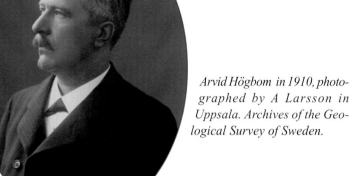

*Arvid Högbom in 1910, photographed by A Larsson in Uppsala. Archives of the Geological Survey of Sweden.*

Sweden is a country whose current nature emerged from a rare changing, practically fantastic geographic development.

Geologist and professor Gerard De Geer wrote this in 1896 in his book *On Scandinavia's geographic development after the Ice Age*. The quote says much about geographic research, not just in Sweden but throughout Europe during the decades leading up to the turn of the 19th century. Geologists emphasised the special features of their own country.

## World Heritage

The shifting of the shoreline is actually a very complex process. It is caused both by the continual uplifting of the land after the melting of the glacial ice sheet (glasio isostasi) and by the changes in sea level (eustasi) caused by climate changes.

After all the disputes between scholars, the final analysis was that Sweden is rising. The theory that became established after the 1910 geologic congress is still the accepted view. The importance of nature quickly became a part of the common cultural heritage through such sources as books on local geography and history used in elementary schools.

In 1909 Sweden's Riksdag established the first national parks, starting with Stora Sjöfallet, Sarek, Garphyttan and Gotska Sandön. In 1984 Skuleskogen National Park was established. In November 2000, the High Coast became a World Heritage Site.

*Vågsfjärden Bay became a lake 150 years ago.*

# The landscape continually challenges me

*AFTER THE SHOWER, OVERLOOK FROM RINGKALLEN*
*Landscape from Nordingrå by Helmer Osslund. (slightly cropped)*

Thage Nordholm was one of the twentieth century's greatest interpreters of the High Coast landscape. He said that the landscape continually challenged him. Its majesty sometimes created a sense of solitude and despair, while sometimes it was ominous and sometimes even liberating. For him, it was a landscape that always fascinated.

Maybe this is why the High Coast has always attracted artists, both before and after Thage Nordholm. They have not always come to paint the landscape. Sometimes they have come to be influenced by it or even to communicate with it, such as in the 1995 art project *In discourse with the landscape*. This project, which also resulted in a book, invited thirteen sculptors to interpret the landscape, both its possibilities and obstacles.

Birgitta Nenzén (1948- ) was raised in Jämtland but now lives in Omne, Nordingrå. She has developed a close and intensive relationship to the High Coast landscape, but she resists portraying it. Her plate metal shields on the rock slabs of Rotsidan are exposed to the wind and water. The shields serve both to protect and as her signature.

## Northern Sweden – a new subject

Helmer Osslund (1866-1938) left his childhood home of Sundsvall for training in the arts in Stockholm and Paris. He was inspired by his teacher Paul Gauguin to use colour fields in clear, bright colours and to interpret the landscape in a more daring way than artists of the 19th century had. Upon returning to Sweden, he travelled north and painted the mountains, the Ångerman River Valley and Nordingrå.

The first time he showed his paintings from northern Sweden in 1898, he received considerable attention. A new subject was opened up for the art public, a daring style that heralded in modernism. Helmer Osslund came to be called northern Sweden's artistic explorer. Prior to Osslund, landscape painters preferred to travel to France. Now many travelled north, particularly during World War I.

The earliest visiting artists to the High Coast did not inspire any local protégés. The hard life based on fishing and farming gave little opportunity for things that were considered the "easy life". The one exception was a poor family in Nora. Erik Svanberg preferred playing an instrument to farming and encouraged his son, Hampe (1883-1961), to pursue his interest in art. Hampe studied at the technical school in Stockholm, today known as the University College of Arts, Crafts and Design, and took study trips abroad. He returned to his home area and settled in Lidebro in Nora parish where he captured the coastal landscape and the daily lives of people in his art. His paintings can still be found throughout the area.

## Artist colony

From the mid-twentieth century, an artist colony developed on the High Coast, primarily in Nordingrå. The colony has gradually grown and offers a rich variety of interpretations of the High Coast. As was the case in the past, most artists spend a few summer months in the area, while some do live in the area year round. Regardless of whether an artist portrays the natural beauty of the area, the hills and valleys, the deep, black lakes, the dark spruce forests, and the boundless lighting of the outer islands serve as inspiration.

Pelle Åberg (1909-1964), a true Stockholmer, was enticed to Nordingrå by fellow painters and bought a place in Björnån. The family became such a part of the area that the son, artist Anders Åberg (1945- ), settled in nearby Häggvik in 1972 and began his life-long project, Mannaminne - "In living memory". Mannaminne combines that which appears to be contradictory - the traditional with the innovative, the domestic with the exotic. The observer is surprised by the daring art and houses from foreign lands, while still feeling at home with the historic buildings and equipment from days gone by in Sweden.

*Birgitta Nenzén's plate metal shields on the rock slabs of Rotsidan are exposed to the wind and water. The shields serve both to protect and as her signature.*

*MOT VÅGSFJÄRDEN (slightly cropped)*
*watercolour by Thage Nordholm*

*The landscape of Ångermanland, particularly around Nordingrå, offers me no peace. At least not in terms of my life as an artist. The lands-cape is continually challenging me. It is however difficult to approach since for me it is so filled with anxiety. Highly-strung and moody.*

*For short periods, however, the lighting can be just right - emotionally speaking - and I might be able to capture something of Nordingrå.*

*Thage Nordholm in the book* MITT NORDINGRÅ.

As a child growing up in Kramfors, Thage Nordholm (1927-1990) would bicycle out to Nordingrå to paint. After the Art Academy in Stockholm, he travelled to the Danish island of Bornholm and the Swedish province of Halland for inspiration. When he began to discover hills in his paintings which he could not find around him, he realised his painting longed for the nature of his childhood. Thage Nordholm bought a place in Stirring in Nordingrå in 1974, where he spent most of his time up until his death.

In the beginning of the 1980s, he created a sensation when he filled the Art Academy's large halls with watercolour landscapes. The Stockholm art community had found Nordingrå and Thage Nordholm was now exhibited in museums.

Siw Thurfjell (1916-1991) came to Nordingrå in the beginning of the 1970s. She became fascinated by the landscape several years before when taking part in a painting class at Pelle Åberggården, a painting school run by a young Anders Åberg and his mother Aina. Siw Thurfjell was a textile artist who worked with silkscreen prints. Her subject was the High Coast landscape, the ceiling paintings at Ulvö Old Chapel and airy motifs with happy people.

## Literature

The earliest descriptions of the province of Ångermanland and the High Coast in literature come from royal officials returning from inspection trips. They often took the land route around the Gulf of Bothnia when travelling between Finland, which belonged to Sweden at the time, and the rest of the kingdom. The dramatic landscape with the threatening Skuleberget Mountain seems to have both attracted and frightened travellers throughout the ages.

> As soon as I came to Ångermanland, the road began to follow large, steep hills, to the point that I almost dared not take them. Wherever I turned, I only saw high hills around me.
>
> Carl von Linné (1707-78) in his book *Lappländsk resa* in 1732.

Selma Lagerlöf (1858-1940) let her character Nils Holgersson look down on Ångermanland from a hilltop and she describes a magnificent landscape.

Ludwig "Lubbe" Nordström (1882-1942) from Härnösand wrote novels about life along the Ångermanland coast. To learn more about daily life in the area, he worked as a fishing hand on Ulvön Island.

> I don't know of any other province in Sweden that is so alive as Ångermanland.
>
> Lubbe Nordström

Kerstin Ekman (1933 - ), takes us into Skuleskogen Forest in the timeless tale of *The Forest of Hours (Rövarna i Skuleskogen).*

> A massive crevice has opened up in one of the hills. The stones have fallen and worn away and left an opening with vertical walls. It is so narrow that two people can stand on opposites sides and have a conversation. No life is visible in its depths, only shadows and rocks.
>
> Kerstin Ekman *The Forest of Hours,* about Slåttdalsskrevan Crevice.

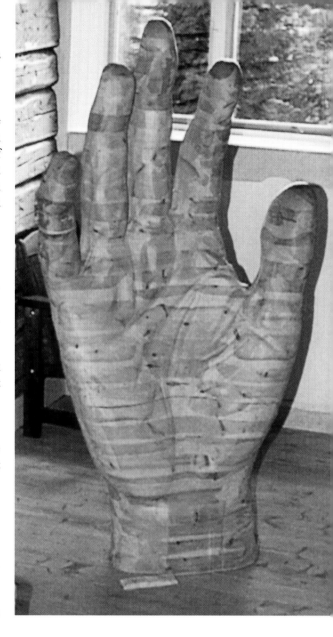

*Anders Åberg settled in Häggvik in 1972 and began his life's work, Mannaminne. Mannaminne combines that which appears to be contradictory - the traditional with the innovative, the domestic with the exotic. The observer is surprised by the daring art and houses from foreign lands, while still feeling at home with the historic buildings and equipment from days gone by in Sweden.*

*The sculpture THE HAND is a self-portrait.*

*At the right*
*Karin Asplund Hesse, Salsåker.*
*This installation was part of the "In discourse with a landscape" project, which invited thirteen sculptors to interpret the landscape, both its possibilities and obstacles.*

Birger Norman (1914-1995) was raised on Svanö Island in the Ångerman River and was active in Stockholm throughout his life. He often described the landscape of his childhood in a similar way as the artist Thage Nordholm. In an article from 1969 about the Ångermanland landscape, his melancholy comes to the fore.

> Blue shadows slide across the Ångermanland hills or lie there unmoved. The thick spruce forests. They reinforce an inevitable melancholy of the soul in anyone born and raised here under the roaming shadows and the muffled song, an organ note, a blues tune. _ _ _ The dual landscape. I carry that which was mine with me. I return every year to that which is. To tell myself that I cannot be here, but this is where I must come. To the coast, to the hilly countryside with fjords, cliffs and heights and with an incomparable light between Skeppsmalen in the north and Hemsö hatt in the south.

*Siw Thurfjell was a textile artist who worked with silkscreen prints. Her subject was the High Coast landscape, the ceiling paintings at Ulvö Old Chapel and airy motifs with happy people.*

# The flora and the rising land

The hilly terrain with peaks above the highest coastline allow the study in a relatively small area of all the different types of vegetation that have been influenced by the rising land. This makes the High Coast unique.

*Till-capped hill in Skuleskogen National Park.*

*The shingle fields south of Slåttdalsmyran.*

The rising land has clearly affected the vegetation below the highest coastline. Till is still found above this line since the Yoldia Sea was not able to wash it away. The till-covered plateau of Skuleberget, which is now more than 286 metres above the sea, is covered with forest. Such till-capped peaks rose out of the water as small islands when the ice melted away. Their height of 300 metres or more above sea level indicates the extent of the uplifting.

The waves washed away the finer material which settled on the seabed. As the land rose, so did the sediment. This has resulted in a division of vegetation into zones, which is most clearly seen in the distribution of the forest. The wide valley floors with the finest sediment have been used for farming. The rich soil in the small valleys and on the lower parts of slopes is covered by a dark green belt of *Spruce* trees, which have their highest growth rate in all of northern Sweden. Higher up, the earth consists of gravel, stones and blocks and the forest is not as dense with more *Pine* and deciduous trees such as *Birch, Aspen, Rowan* and *Goat Willow*. The shingle fields are barren with the occasional shrivelled spruces or dwarf pines. Several hundred year old pines, often knotted and twisted, grow on the hill plateaus. The oldest are more than 500 years old.

The outer edges of the shores are often steep and rocky. This is not a hospitable environment for plants that attempt to establish themselves. The 8 mm annual uplifting has a greater visible affect on the flat beaches, but is less noticeable on steeper shorelines. The ability of plants to spread is lessened by the naturally

shifting water levels, storms and erosion from the winter ice. An unusually powerful winter storm can wash away several years of growth in a shore zone so that the plants have to begin again. Seed-bearing annual plants have a particularly hard time establishing themselves. Perennials, such as sedge hybrids and grasses which primarily spread through shooting roots and sprouts at ground level, do better. About 10 years are needed to see a lasting effect of the rising land on the vegetation.

## Cut off lakes
A visible effect of the rising land is the gradual cutting off of bays with shallow openings so that they become lakes. Along these new lakes, plants dependent on brackish water and maritime plants move further out toward the sea as access to salt water decreases. Some species can survive as relics from the time before the sea was cut off. Åvikefjärden and Bäckfjärden in Nätra are examples of this process.

## Shell Sediments
Layers of sediment made up primarily of crushed mussel shells, have risen with the land and now provide nutrients to the local flora. Such sediments occur up to 80 metres above the sea. Surface water and ground water that seep through the shell sediment are enriched with calcium and nourish the marshes, damp forests and other soils. These areas favour orchids and other species that are more or less dependent on calcium and offer wild flower enthusiasts plenty to see.

In some areas where the bedrock consists of easily crumbled dolerite, anorthosite or gabbro, there is a rich selection of plants. These types of rocks have a certain amount of calcium, but lower than in the shell sediments.

## Alpine flora
When the glacial ice sheet retreated from the coast 9600 years ago, the uplift was 10 to 15 centimetres a year and the edge of the ice pulled back at times more than 300 metres a year. Alpine vegetation quickly established itself on the ice-free islands and along the coast, but the period with an alpine climate was short. The temperature had already begun to rise as a warning of the coming warmer period. It can be assumed that lichen, different types of shrubs, *Dwarf Birch*, *Willow*, *Mountain Avens* and *Purple Saxifrage* were among the first immigrants for a few hundred years. Soon, *Birch*, *Aspen* and *Pine* moved in. Pollen studies have shown that *Sea-buckthorn*, *Goosefoots* and *Mugwort* grew along the shores.

Soon the temperature rose to a level that was too high for the alpine plants. Seven genuine alpine species, however, have managed to survive, most in shadowy cracks in the High Coast's steep cliffs. The most extreme is *Purple Saxifrage* which is only found on Själandsklinten's and Ringkalleberget's high, northerly dolerite cliffs, 200 metres above the sea. These are their only locations east of the mountains.

## Warm climate flora
The landscape changed radically when the warmer period arrived. *Alder* migrated from the south and took over the coastal forests. Thick deciduous forests with *Wych Elm*, *Norway Maple*, *Small-leaved Lime*, *Hazel* (probably even *Oak*) and a rich flora of southern, warm-weather plants spread north and reached all the way

The mixture of species in such a variety of settings reflects the history of plant migration as the climate changed after the Ice Age and people settled the area. Compared with other areas in the world, the flora in Scandinavia is very young - less than 15,000 years.

*Vågsfjärden Bay is now a lake that was cut off from the sea. It is one metre above sea level.*

*Raised beach on shingle field at a former bay in Skuleskogen National Park. The entrance to the bay rose above sea level, forming a lake. The lake then filled in creating a marsh, 200 metres above sea level.*

*Previous pages*
*Animal life in the High Coast wilderness.*
*Three-toed woodpecker, Lynx, and Moose.*

*The flora is lush, particularly where deciduous trees grow. Amylocystis Lapponica, Baneberry, Coralroot, Lady's slipper, Ghost Orchid, Early Marsh - orchid with the beetle Trichius fasciatus and the lichen Usnea longissima.*

*Hazel*

*Purple Saxifrage*

*Both alpine plants and plants from southern latitudes have found safe havens in sheltered areas on steep hills. Holly-ferns stand side-by-side with Maple, Hazel, and Spring Vetchling in high steep areas of Ringkalleberget's north-east side, and Purple Saxifrage and Tufted Saxifrage grow in the rocky crevices. This is unique for the High Coast and an ecologically interesting combination of plants.*

to the Gulf of Bothnia's coastline. This warmer period, with higher humidity and 2 to 3 degrees warmer average temperature than the present, lasted about 3000 years, between 8000 and 5000 years ago. The climate then began to gradually cool and the southerly flora was pushed back. In small, protected valleys and on the southern slopes of hills where the cold north winds could not reach, it is still possible to find remains of the multitude of plants from warmer periods, such as deciduous trees like *Maple* and *Lime* and northern outposts of *Yellow Star-of-Bethlehem, Prickly Sedge, Coralroot, Spring Vetchling, Golden-saxifrage, Hedge Woundwort, Peach-leaved Bellflower, Wall Lettuce* and many others. On about a dozen southern slopes, the *Hazel* has defied the cooler climate. It grows on the upper edge of steep slopes where the rocks have given way and the sun-heated cliffs stay warm even during cold nights. On these spots, the snow settles later and melts earlier than in other areas so the growth period is longer. This has meant that over 40 plant species have been able to maintain their northernmost positions along the coast. The two hills with the largest number of southerly species are the well-known Skuleberget Mountain by the E4 highway in Vibyggerå and Omneberget in Nordingrå. Omneberget's southern slope with its deciduous forest is the only place at this latitude where it is possible to hike in a real *Hazel grove* carpeted by *Liverleafs* and *Wood Anemones* in early spring.

### The Spruce spreads - northern forest flora
The temperature began to decrease even more 3000 years ago. The climate became more accommodating to the *Spruce* which began to expand its territory. A dark green cover of spruce forest spread and forced out deciduous forests, but not everywhere. There is often a richer variety of plants in forests that are not too dense and that have deciduous trees.

Typical plants for the taiga moved in, such as sedge, *Carex disperma*, *Alpine Blue-sow-thistle* and the spruce forest's beautiful *Calypso Orchid*, which flowers at the end of May or beginning of June.

*Calypso Orchids* require rich soil, preferably with calsium, which the High Coast has plenty of with its mussel shell deposits. This is also true for the *Ghost Orchid*, another sought-after orchid that flowers two months after the *Calypso*.

Most sites with an abundance of species that require calsium from the shell sediments are shadowy spruce and mixed forests. A sure sign of rich soil is often a plentiful layer of *Liverleaf*. Some really demanding species are the *Rattlesnake Fern* and a number of orchids, such as *Calypso Orchid, Ghost Orchid, Common Twayblade, Bird's-nest Orchid, Lady's Slipper, One-leaved Bog-orchid* and *Narrow-leaved Marsh-orchid*. The last two grow in marshes. *Broad-leaved Cottongrass, Early Marsh-orchids* and *Bog Orchids* are more common and can be found in the coastal marshes with a supply of calsium.

### Immigrants from west and east
Immigrants from other directions also meet on the High Coast. The *Northern Rock-cress's* white tufts are common near shorelines on both rocky and sandy beaches between Härnön and Skags Udde. This is the High Coast World Heritage's greatest botanical attraction since it is not found anywhere else in our country. It probably came from the Norwegian coast and over the mountains shortly after the glacial ice sheet melted from the mountains.

The beaches are often rocky with little vegetation where the *Northern Rock-cress* grows together with the *Alpine Catchfly* which is more common here than

anywhere else along Sweden's coasts. They are in good company with *Reflexed Saltmarsh-grass*, *Round-fruited Rush* and *Procumbent Pearlwort*. All these species enjoy the advantages of the rising land which continually creates new environments with little competition from other vegetation.

A stately plant is the white variety of the *Giant Bellflower* that decorates the High Coast's wooden slopes and ravines. Otherwise, its home is along the Atlantic coast and it likely made its way here during the last warm period. A species that came from the east is the rare and elegant grass *Cinna latifolia* in the shadowy confines of the Slåttdalsklyftan Crevice.

There are also many lichens and mosses that follow the same pattern of immigration and several oceanic mosses and lichens grow in the Skuleskogen Forest's highland regions with higher humidity. The lichen *Rhizocarpon Geographicum* is also common here.

## The work of humans

As people moved in, they brought with them new plants that thrived around settlements. Meadows that were traditionally kept clear through hay-making and grazing had an abundance of wildflowers. As farming has become more mechanised, these meadows are increasingly rare. In sunny coastal areas, there is still a large variety of plant species particular to settled areas and warmer climates. *Moonwort* grows here and *Downy Oat-grass*, *Maiden Pink*, *Nottingham Catchfly*, *Alpine*

*The Northern Rock-cress and the common Lyme-grass. Razorbills breed in the High Coast.*

*Cinquefoil, Field Gentian, Breckland Thyme, Lady's Bedstraw, Peach-leaved Bellfloweer, Brown Knapweed* and *Spotted Cat's-ear* all flower here.

Dry meadow hills around settlements and chapels in old fishing villages along the High Coast are of particular interest. Fishermen from the south spent summers here from the 16th to the 20th centuries. They may have contributed spring flowers from southern reaches such as *Common Whitlowgrass*, *Strict Forget-me-not*, *Spring Speedwell*, *White Stonecrop*, and the yellow whitlowgrass *Draba nemorosa*.

*A young Tengmalms owl in Skuleskogen National Park. The deep whistles of Tengmalm owls can be heard up to three kilometres away.*

Major excavations of Iron Age farms in Lappnäset (600 to 900 AD) and Gallsätter (250 to 700 AD) were conducted when the High Coast Bridge and the subsequent new passage for E4 were built. Iron Age houses were large, between 18 and 24 metres long. The farmers and the animals each lived in their own part of the longhouse, with a storage area on the short side. In Lappnäset, the graves were close to the house, which was common for this period. There are also remains from ancient fields, iron production and weaving. With the advent of permanent buildings and fields that required work also came

*The longhouse in Gene was nearly 40 metres long. It has now been reconstructed based on the archaeological findings and offers a unique opportunity to see an Iron Age home.*

*None of the Iron Age farms and graves have been found lower than 20 metres above today's sea level.*

*1829*

*20th century*

the need to declare land ownership rights. The graves of ancestors were important markers for this reason.

The hillfort at Rödklitten in Nordingrå is an additional expression of the will of Iron Age people to defend their land and their settlements against invaders. Rödklitten is also the area from which some of the red slate-like sandstone used to make the T-shaped tools in Överveda came from.

## Centralised power in the Middle Ages

Antiquity is considered to have come to an end with the introduction of Christianity around 1050. This was the transition to the Middle Ages. The large longhouses from the Iron Age disappeared with the onset of the Middle Ages, and were replaced by smaller log farm buildings, each with its specific use. A farm that has been in continual use from the Iron Age and the Middle Ages is Arnäsbacken just past the church in Arnäs. One of the log buildings is dated to the 900s.

As the Church became increasingly influential, so did ideas from mainland Europe. The church in Grundsunda is an example of how the Church's power and the king's administration went hand in hand. A trading centre was established here in the 13th century and the construction of a stone church began. The importance of the site is reflected in the fact that a bishop's ring was found here. Remains of a Middle Ages church can be seen in Nordingrå, and Nora Church has a baptism font from the workshop of the Gotlandic master Calcinarius.

*Piles of pitch wood were left on high points within sight of each other so that they could be lit to warn of approaching enemies. The peaks of the High Coast were an important link in this warning system.*

*The labyrinths on rock slabs and outer islands could be interpreted as a grass-roots silent protest against the increasingly centralised powers. There are twelve labyrinths along the High Coast.*
*County Museum Härnösand.*

State and church taxes were paid in the form of skins, seal blubber, salmon, Baltic herring and linen material. A royal domain was established in Kungsgården in Bjärtrå by the Ångerman River. This included a Middle Ages stronghold made of wood that has been dated to the winter of 1428, using the tree rings in the well-preserved logs.

The coastal population sold their own goods and purchased new goods on sailing trips along the coast. To ensure that it could collect toll fees, the State founded the town of Härnösand in 1585 so that trade would take place within the confines of a city. Even so, coastal fishing and sailing trips continued to be difficult to control.

The fascinating stone labyrinths on rock slabs and outer islands could be interpreted as a grassroots silent protest to the increasingly centralised powers. Or perhaps they were related to navigation or to magical rituals intended to ensure good fishing and favourable weather.

## Fishing villages, agriculture and summer farms

As early as the 15th century, the merchants in Gävle, a town 300 kilometres to the south, realised that the summer fishing on the High Coast was a valuable and untapped resource. Every summer, they sailed their boats filled with supplies, linen, goats, pigs, children and servants to the fishing villages on the High Coast. Barsta, Bönhamn, Norrfällsviken, Trysunda, Ulvön were all *summer homes* for Gävle fishermen. In 1557 the merchants in Gävle were granted sole rights to fish along all of northern Sweden's coast for a fee of every tenth barrel of fish. In 1772 this right was repealed and fishing in the sea once again became a right of everyone. Local area people began to use the fishing villages themselves and eventually many stayed on permanently. Since the 1950s, fishing has declined in importance and the old fishing villages have become summer homes for holiday seekers.

Originally, each family had its own living quarters and boathouse. Even today, this is a common trait of the region. During the 17th and 18th centuries, chapels were built and the summer's Sundays were devoted to religious meditation. During the winter, the chapels, which were owned by their congregations, had a more practical function as storage places for nets and fishing equipment.

Fishing has always been important, particularly during the Middle Ages when the Catholic rules for fasting were strict. The High Coast is best known for its fermented Baltic Herring, which was noted as early as the 16th century.

*Baltic Herring workers in front of a boathouse in Ulvöhamn Harbour.*
*Örnsköldsvik Museum Archive.*

*The abandoned fishing village of Sandviken on northern Ulvön Island ended up away from the shoreline because of the rising land.*

*Ulvö Chapel, built 1622, is northern Sweden's oldest fisherman's chapel. The paintings are from 1719 and illustrate biblical fishing scenes with people in 18th century clothing.*

Agriculture with animal husbandry was the main source of income for the people along the High Coast. There was limited land to expand onto because of the hilly landscape. It was possible, however, to increase grazing lands by using summer farms. There are many summer farms and pastures preserved along the High Coast. The summer farms Skrattabborrtjärn in Skuleskogen Forest and Fjärdbotten in Nora are interesting places to visit. Summer farms were similar of the fishing villages and served as an important source of additional food and money. In comparison to the fishing villages, though, the summer farms were characterised as work places for women. Cheese and butter making were important sources of income. When the

population increased dramatically in the 18th and 19th centuries, summer farms, together with coastal fishing and the growing sawmill industry, were a resource that allowed for the expansion.

## Sami on the High Coast

If the permanent population was characterised by an unstable life, this was even more the case with the Sami (formerly known as Laplanders) population. The reindeer grazing lands in Nordingrå appear to be ancient and the Sami have likely been here as long as they have been a distinct group of people.

*Semi-nomadic Sami from Vilhelmina Northern Sami Village in front of the church in Arnäs on the High Coast.*
*Örnsköldsvik Museum Archive.*

Many place names in the area point to Sami connections. The plentiful supply of lichen along the High Coast provides excellent reindeer grazing.

During the 18th century, mainly forest-dwelling Sami from the inland regions of Ångermanland Province came to the High Coast. Later, the mountain Sami from the Vilhelmina northern and southern Sami villages arrived. Since the reindeer kept to the lichen-rich forests, their winter grazing was not an issue with the farmers. Conflicts between the Sami and the farmers were no greater than what was normal between the farmers themselves. There were also non-nomadic Sami living on the High Coast.

*At the right*
*Farm house with door by the sculptor Pehr Westman in Kåsta on the High Coast.*

*As soon as we begin speaking about time along the High Coast, we are also referring to the level above the sea. We can determine the age of a coastal settlement by measuring its height above the sea.*

## Timeline

The combination of farming, hunting, fishing and seal hunting developed as early as the Bronze Age and continues to this day, even if the importance of the catches is much diminished. Handcrafts and other side sources of income have developed into today's small industries.

The crackvalleys that formed in the bedrock allowed the rivers to reach the sea, thus permitting the floating of logs from the inland to the coast for the wood industry. The wood industry, in turn, allowed today's modern Västernorrland County to develop and set the stage for the industrialisation of the entire country. The sawmill in Äskja in Ullånger is the only one within the World Heritage Site that is still in use. The sawmills in Lugnvik and Bollstabruk and the pulp factories and papermills in Utansjö, Väja-Dynäs, Alfredshem and Husum symbolise today's large-scale production.

The landscape that formed through the forces of nature and the actions of people since the Stone Age can still be found throughout the World Heritage Site. Geologic formations and the remains of past people create a timeline that can be followed in the landscape and which illustrates the connections through the ages.

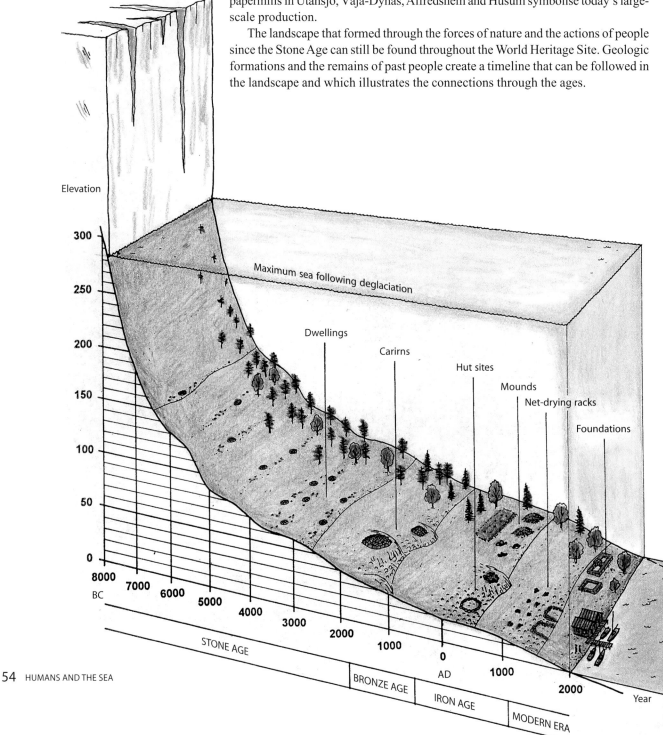

# Protected areas

*The High Coast shines blue when the hills and spruce forests give way to the sky and sea.*

*Protecting a sufficiently large area of the High Coast's nature was one of the prerequisites for being named a World Heritage Site.*

**Skuleskogen National Park** was inaugurated in 1984. The park has nearly 3000 hectares. To reach the park's southern entrance, follow the signs from E4 at Skuleberget Mountain. Follow the signs from E4 at the restaurant "Näske krog" for the northern entrance. From the parking area, there are 30 kilometres of marked trails to such destinations as the bay of Kälaviken, Slåttdalsskrevan Crevice, the Näske summer farm, and the tarn Skrattabborrtjärnen. The park also has cabins where hikers can spend the night. Information about the High Coast Hiking Trail, which cuts through the park, is available at Skule Naturum.

Skuleskogen Forest is a highland wilderness area. It resembles an old-growth forest and alternates between marshes, shoreline, ravines, deep crevices, rocky slopes, shingle fields, wave-washed rock slabs, and till-capped peaks above what is known as the highest coastline. Högsvedjeberget stands nearly 350 metres above the sea. One of the most interesting geologic sights is the 200-metre long and 40-metre deep Slåttdalsskrevan Crevice. The bedrock has occurrences of magmatic

rocks such as dolerite. Beautiful Bronze Age cairn graves can be seen above the Näske summer farm.

The variety of species and environments in the national park is amazing. The flora is a mixture of native plants and others that have moved into the area from all directions of the compass. *Liverleaf* is common on fertile soils. *Wood Fescue*, close to its northern most limit, is found on southern slopes above Kälaviken, *Hazel* grows in Slåttdalsskrevan Crevice and the country's northernmost native *Maples* are found a bit further north.

*Lynxes* live in Skuleskogen Forest's isolated areas and there is a large *Moose* population. All species of woodpecker common in northern Sweden are found in the area's forests. The *Grey-headed Woodpecker* prefers aspen stands. Birds of prey, such as *Goshawks* and *Buzzards*, can find plenty of places to build their nests. Several species of birds that are normally found further north and inland live in the area, such as *Willow Grouse, Waxwings, Siberian Jays* and *Rustic Buntings*.

*Old-growth forest in Skuleskogen National Park.*

*Skuleberget Mountain*

*Fishing village at Skags Udde*

*Ghost Orchids*

*View from Balesudden*

**Skuleberget Nature Reserve** is located next to E4; turn off at Skule Naturum and Skuleberget Camping. There is a climbing trail to the cave on the east slope and a chair lift to the top from the western side.

The 295-metre high Skuleberget Mountain is a till-capped hill. At the top above the wave-washed rock slabs, visitors can walk along the world's highest post-glacial coastline, 286 metres above the sea, and the forest-covered till cap above. Even though the steep face of Skuleberget Mountain is not toward the south, it still has one of the High Coast's richest varieties of plants that normally are found in more southerly latitudes. *Hazel, Maple* and *Lime* are among the deciduous trees in the reserve. Many of the southern species are primarily found at the top edge of loose-soil slopes, north of the trail to the caves. These include *Sticky Catchfly, Copse-bindweed, Hairy Rock-cress, Mountain Currant, Dog-rose, Perforate St. John's-wort, Teesdale Violet, Basil Thyme, Fly Honeysuckle* and *Peach-leaved Bellflowers.*

**Skags Udde.** Turn off E4 12 kilometres north of Örnsköldsvik and head toward Skeppsmalen. Drive 17 kilometres to the parking area at the idyllic fishing village of Skeppsmalen, with its chapel from the 19th century. Walk to the lighthouse at the end of the point that juts out to the south in the Gulf of Bothnia.

The smooth wave-washed rock that was lifted from the sea by the rising land has a beautiful pattern that clearly shows glacial striae made by the ice. This is best seen from the lighthouse and on the rock hill west of the chapel. The harbour is a good example of how a lake is formed from a bay. The entrance to the harbour is becoming shallower as the land rises.

The flora on the dry meadows and along the roads is typical for High Coast fishing villages and is a rich mix of plants brought from other areas by the people who settled here. Many of these flower earlier in the spring than the native plants of the area. This includes *Common Whitlowgrass,* the whitlowgrass *Draba nemorosa, Strict Forget-me-not* and some rarities such as *Daisy-leaf Grape-fern* and *White Stonecrop.* Skags Udde is an excellent place to observe migrating birds during the spring and autumn.

**Ögeltjärnen Nature Reserve** is found 2 kilometres south-west of the Gullvik beach area. Follow the signs from the beach or the car park along the Tallstigen Trail to the lake and then to the top of Ögeltjärnberget to enjoy the view of the coast.

Judging by the rich flora, the marshes and marsh forests to the south of the lake are enriched by shell deposits. *Hair Sedge,* which indicates the presence of calsium, grows in the marshes. *Liverleaf* in the spruce and deciduous forest indicates rich soil and many bushes that require an abundance of nutrients grow here, including *Mountain Currant, Mezereon* and *Guelder-rose.* Orchids include the *Frog Orchid,* the *Common Twayblade* and the *Ghost Orchid.*

**Balesudden Nature Reserve** is a peninsula 4 kilometres east of the village of Köpmanholmen. From Köpmanholmen, drive to Hålviken. Follow the trail marked with signs into the reserve to visit Balestjärnen and Balesberget. From the north, the reserve is reached by way of Utby at Bäckfjärden Bay heading towards Bäck. There is a parking area at Sandlågan from where the marked trail begins heading south. The High Coast Hiking Trail goes through the reserve.

The reserve offers different types of hiking through relatively untouched spruce forest and deciduous-evergreen forest with very hilly terrain. Interesting geologic sights include shingles fields, giant pot-holes and a hard rock stack. *Alpine Catchfly,*

Common Spotted-orchids and *Mezereons* grow by the stream that is fed from the crystal clear waters of the mystical Balestjärnen Lake. This small lake is probably enriched with calsium from shell deposits. The reserve offers a wonderful overlook of the World Heritage coast. An unusually large *Alder* with multiple trunks and a lower trunk circumference of 5.5 metres is found at Bodviken.

*Trysunda fishing village*

**Trysunda and Skrubban Nature Reserves**. Visitors can take a ferry from Köpmanholmen to Trysunda, where they can hike the trails around the island. On calm days, visitors can reach the island of Skrubban by boat.

The island of Trysunda is made up of rapakivi granite, sandstone and dolerite. The fishing village has a history that goes back to the Gävle fishermen's time. There is also a chapel from the 17th century. The rich flora in the meadows around settlements and the chapel is typical for fishing villages along the High Coast. There are interesting dolerite formations on the south-east side of the island by Storviken. The decorative *Forked Spleenwort* fern grows in the crevices.

The steep, wild cliffs on Skrubban are made of column-like dolerite and are difficult to climb. The area called Skrubbfjället on the west side of the island is a depression in the steep cliffs from where visitors can climb to the top of the island on calm days. *Angular Solomon's-seal*, *Liverleaf* and *Mezereon* grow on shell sediment on the slope. *Tufted Saxifrage*, *Alpine Catchfly* and *Northern Rockcress* have gained a foothold in the dolerite walls facing the sea. In spite of the island's difficult terrain, *Moose*, *Foxes* and *Mountain Hares* inhabit it at times.

*Tufted Saxifrage*

**Herrestaberget Nature Reserve** is beside the road to Östmarkum in the village of Herresta, on the west side of Gällstasjön Lake. A trail starts at the village of Sätra.

The reserve has cliffs to the east and south and the northernmost occurrences of *Spring Vetchling* and *Woodruff*. Relics from colder climates grow on the steep slopes, such as *Tufted Saxifrage* and an alpine form of *Blue Fleabane*, which can be seen on the shaded easterly cliff by the edge of the road.

**Stormyran Nature Reserve** is on the north-eastern side of northern Ulvön Island. Hike across the land south from the Norrbyn-Sandviken road where it passes Sandvikssjön Lake.

This is an untouched marsh area enriched with dolerite and maybe even shell sediments. Open marsh areas have a red glow from the *Oblong-leaved Sundew* that grows in tight carpets on the ground. Other marsh plants that indicate fertile conditions are *Brown Beak-sedge*, *Broad-leaved Cottongrass*, *Early Marsh-orchid* and *Bog Orchid*. In some years, Bog Orchids flower in the thousands.

*Ripe Cloudberries*

**Södra Ulvön and Marviksgrunnan**. Transport is available by boat to Marviksgrunnan on the western side or to Ulvösundet Sound on the island's northern side, from where the trail to Marviksgrunnan starts. The island's south-eastern section is a nature reserve.

The landscape is characterised by barren flat slabs of rock and shingle fields with wind-worn pines and spruce. Coniferous forests are dominated by spruce. The bedrock is primarily dolerite, but on the east side there is also red rapakivi granite. The volcanic dolerite benefits more demanding plant species normally found at southern latitudes, such as *Liverleaf*, *Mountain Currant*, *Dog-rose* and *Fly Honeysuckle*. The village of Marviksgrunnan, with its chapel next to the reserve, has a typical meadow flora for old High Coast fishing villages, such as *Common Whitlowgrass* and *Strict Forget-me-not*.

*Wood Sandpiper on Södra Ulvön Island*

*Mjältön Nature Reserve*

*Liverleaf*

**Gnäggen Nature Reserve** is a bird island south of the Ulvöarna islands with colonies of *Razorbills* and *Guillemots*. Trespassing is forbidden at all times of the year.

**Mjältön** is Sweden's highest island at 236 metres above the sea. The island's nature reserve is a 600-metre wide belt through the centre of the island. There are places to anchor boats in the protected Baggviken Bay or the dock at Sundsbodarna. Trails take visitors from Baggviken to the top of the island and down to Sundsbodarna.

The island is primarily made of rapakivi granite. The peak of Bastutoberget has one of the most spectacular overlooks of the World Heritage coast. The lush vegetation by Baggviken and Baggtjärnen indicate that the underlying soil is enriched by shell sediments. It is easy to find *Alpine Catchfly* and *Northern Rock-cress* on the rocky beaches.

**Villmyran Nature Reserve** is 2 kilometres north-west of Norrfällsviken. Follow the signs from the Mjällom-Norrfällsviken road. The trail starts at the car park. Note that the trail system is not marked and the vegetation in the area is easily damaged if trampled upon.

Hikers walk through an impressive and lush spruce forest on the northern slope toward Ullångersfjärden Bay. The flora benefits from shell sediment in depressions between the banks of the old shores. In addition to *Liverleaf, Wood Vetch, Peach-leaved Bellflower, Wall Lettuce* and other plants, there are also twelve types of orchids in the area. The most interesting attraction is the *Calypso*

*Orchid*, which flowers in the dark spruce forests in the beginning of June, the earliest of all the orchids in the World Heritage Site. Two months later, in August, the pale and mystical *Ghost Orchid* flowers. This plant lacks chlorophyll.

**Storsand Nature Reserve** is an area with dunes and beaches barely 2 kilometres north of Norrfällsviken Fishing Village. Follow the signs from Norrfällsviken to the car park in the pine forest south of the beach, which is perfect for swimming.

The area has large sand dunes, which is rare for the High Coast. East of the sandy beach is a somewhat rocky beach that has the High Coast's most exclusive plant, the *Northern Rock-cress*.

*Northern Rock-cress, Storsand Nature Reserve*

**Norrfällsviken Nature Reserve** covers the peninsula south-east of the fishing village, where the car park is located. The marked trails take hikers to the large shingle fields that stretch all the way down to the shore.

Rock slabs with occasional pines dominate the area. The flora by the village and the old chapel just outside of the reserve is typical for High Coast fishing villages. Many of the plants flower early in the spring, such as *Common Whitlowgrass*, the whitlowgrass *Draba nemorosa* and *Strict Forget-me-not*.

*Norrfällsviken shingle field*

**Omneberget Nature Reserve** is a south-facing hill on the north side of the lake Omnesjön. Turn at the Omnebadet swimming area and follow the marked trail through the reserve's woods on the hill's south side.

Except for Skuleberget Mountain, Omneberget has the richest collection of plants more typical of latitudes to the south. There are over fifty southerly species. Hikers on the south slope walking through the deciduous forest with *Maple* and *Hazel* might think they are in south Sweden. The area's only real stand of *Hazel* is found here with carpets of *Liverleaf* and *Wood Anemone*. The *Broad-leaved Helleborine* orchid, which only grows in a few spots in the Heritage site and which is at its northernmost limit, is found here. Hikers may hear songbirds such as the *Wood Warbler*, the *Blackcap* and the *Scarlet Grosbeak*.

*Southern slope of Omneberget*

**Halsviksravinen Nature Reserve** is 1 kilometre west of Rävsön. Follow the signs at the foot of a steep hill on the road from Tollsäter toward Rävsön. Park above Halsviksmyran Marsh, just south of the ravine or by the forest road above the ravine's western slope. There is a marked trail from the forest road down the slope to the beach.

This deep stream-cut ravine resembles an old-growth forest with large *Spruce* stands and deciduous trees such as occasional *Maples*. The soil is enriched by dolerite and most likely with shell sediment. Interesting plants for the area are *Wood Fescue, Coralroot, Spring Vetchling, Hedge Woundwort, Fly Honeysuckle, Woodruff* and *Bird's-nest Orchid*, which is exceedingly rare this far north. *Ghost Orchids* also grow here, and the Halsviksmyran Marsh has such rarities as *Narrow-leaved Marsh-orchids* and *One-leaved Bog-orchids*. The stately *Giant Bellflower* also grows here. Birds, such as *Grey-headed Woodpeckers, Three-toed Woodpeckers, Wrens, Blackcaps* and *Wood Warblers*, like the old-growth deciduous forest. Sometimes, visitors can hear the songs of the *Red-breasted Flycatcher,* the *Icterine Warbler* and the *Greenish Warbler*.

*Ostrich Ferns in Halsviksravinen*

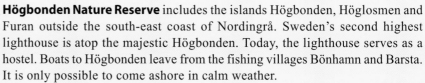

*Högbonden and its hostel*

*Rotsidan*

*Sandstone on Storön Island*

**Högbonden Nature Reserve** includes the islands Högbonden, Höglosmen and Furan outside the south-east coast of Nordingrå. Sweden's second highest lighthouse is atop the majestic Högbonden. Today, the lighthouse serves as a hostel. Boats to Högbonden leave from the fishing villages Bönhamn and Barsta. It is only possible to come ashore in calm weather.

The island's barren dolerite rocks with cracks and caves host little vegetation. *Reflexed Saltmarsh-grass*, *Rounded-fruited Rush*, *Alpine Catchfly* and the High Coast's botanical attraction - the *Northern Rock-cress*, grow on the rocky shores. Höglosmen is a breeding island for gulls.

**Rotsidan Nature Reserve** is a slab rock area that encompasses a 4-kilometre stretch of the south-eastern coast. Take the road north from Fällsvik and turn at the sign. There is a car park and trail with handicap access.

There is easy hiking on the flat rock slabs with cracks and boulders along the shore. The rock is dolerite. There is only sparse vegetation, but it is plentiful in the crevices and cracks in the rocks and includes the low-growing *Northern Rock-cress*. This plant has rosettes of tongue-shaped and slightly jagged leaves and white flowers. It is easily mistaken for other white flowers found in similar eco-systems – the *Common Marsh-bedstraw* and the *Knotted Pearlwort*, but these have different types of leaves. Rotsidan offers an exciting outdoor experience throughout the year.

**Storön Nature Reserve** is accessed by boat from Hemsön or Berghamn.

The bedrock is dolerite and sandstone with dramatic formations at its southern point. Gammhamnen, an old fishing village in a sheltered bay, was abandoned in the 1870s when the bay was cut off from the sea by the uplifting land. *Liverleaf*, *Baneberry*, *Mezereon*, *Coniferous Bedstraw*, *Guelder-rose* and *Fly Honeysuckle* grow in depressions and on slopes away from the shore. The *Northern Rock-cress* grows on sandstone at the southern point.

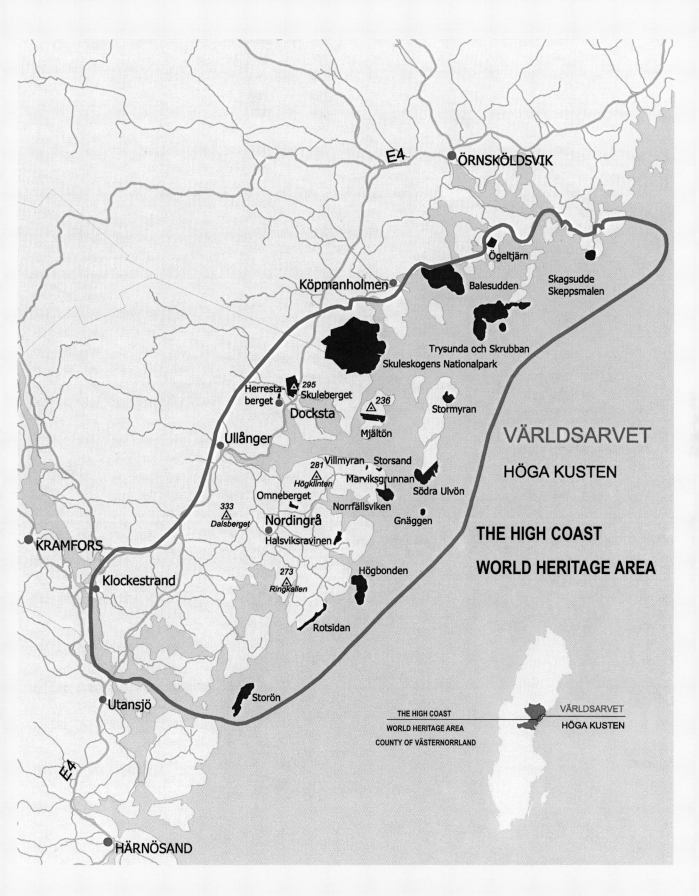

E4

● ÖRNSKÖLDSVIK

Köpmanholmen ●

Ögeltjärn

Balesudden

Skagsudde
Skeppsmalen

Trysunda och Skrubban

Skuleskogens Nationalpark

Herresta-
berget ● △ *295*
Skuleberget

Docksta

△ *236*
Mjältön

Stormyran

Ullånger ●

*281*
Villmyran  Storsand
△
*Högklinten*  Marviksgrunnan

Södra Ulvön

Omneberget
*333*  Norrfällsviken  Gnäggen
△
*Dalsberget*  Nordingrå

Halsviksravinen

● KRAMFORS

Klockestrand  *273*
△
*Ringkallen*

Högbonden

Rotsidan

Storön

● Utansjö

VÄRLDSARVET

HÖGA KUSTEN

THE HIGH COAST

WORLD HERITAGE AREA

THE HIGH COAST
WORLD HERITAGE AREA
COUNTY OF VÄSTERNORRLAND

VÄRLDSARVET
HÖGA KUSTEN

E4

● HÄRNÖSAND

# Finding your way on the High Coast

We recommend that you visit one of the area's tourist offices to make your visit to the High Coast World Heritage Site more enjoyable. The tourist office staff can help answer your questions and provide maps, directions and information about accommodations, dining, events and organised activities. The High Coast is easily accessible from European Highway E4.

### Kramfors Tourist Office
Torggatan 2
S-872 80 Kramfors
tel: +46-612-80120, fax: +46-612-10784
e-mail: turistinfo@kramfors.se
website: www.kramfors.se
Open year round.

### Örnsköldsvik Tourist Office
Nygatan 18
S-891 88 Örnsköldsvik
tel: +46-660-88100, fax: +46-660-8812
e-mail: turism@ornskoldsvik.se
website: www.ornskoldsvik.se
Open year round.

### Skule Naturum
Skule Naturum is located at the foot of Skuleberget Mountain. It serves as a combination tourist and information centre. The entrance to the Skuleberget Mountain Nature Reserve and the start of the Skuleberget climbing trail are both here. Visitors can take the chairlift from Docksta to the top of the mountain at 295 metres above sea level.
e-mail: skulenaturum@y.lst.se
tel: +46-613-40171, fax: +46-613-40424
Open year round.

### The High Coast Bridge
Hornöberget, tourist information for Ångermanland Province
Hotel, restaurant and information.
tel: +46-613-50480
Open year round.

### Mitt Sverige Turism
Norra kyrkogatan 15
S-871 32  Härnösand
tel: +46-611-557750, fax: +46-611-22107
e-mail: info@mittsverigeturism.se
website: www.upplevmittsverige.nu
Open year round.

**Västernorrland County Administrative Board**
S-871 86 Härnösand
tel: +46-611-34 90 00
website: www.y.lst.se
Website for the World Heritage Site:   www.highcoast.net

*The evening sun on Slåttdalsberget in Skuleskogen National Park offers a place where effects of time and the beauty of the moment combine to sooth the soul.*

# Places to discover

### Skuleskogen National Park

Hike with a view of the sea and archipelago through the impressive Slåttdalsskrevan Crevice and see the till-capped hills covered with forest above the highest coastline. Skuleskogen National Park offers a system of clearly marked trails. Old farmer trials and horse trails that are easy to follow start in Kälaviken and Näske. See pages 56 - 57.

### Nature reserves

See pages 58 - 65.

### The High Coast Hiking Trail

This 130-kilometre trail starts at the High Coast Bridge or the town centre in Örnsköldsvik. The trail passes farms, forests, overlooks, fishing villages, summer farms, sandy beaches and much more.

### Gene Iron Age Village

This active farm from the late Iron Age has been built based on the findings from archaeological sites in the area. Open year round for groups. Make reservations in advance. Activities every day in the summer. tel: +46-660-53710

### Trysunda and Ulvöarna islands by ferry

Learn about the High Coast World Heritage Site from sea level. See the effects the uplifting land has had on the fishing village Sandviken. Sandviken is most easily reached by bicycle, which can be hired in Ulvöhamn harbour. Visit the lovely chapel from the 17th century. The ferry leaves from Köpmanholmen.
For reservations, call: +46-660-12537, 224093

*Skiing in Skuleskogen National park*
*Slåttdalsberget and the archipelago*
*Högbonden Lighthouse*
*Fishing in Nordingrå*

## Högbonden Lighthouse

The lighthouse keeper's house on Högbonden island is a popular hostel where visitors can spend the night. Limited dining available. The ferry to Högbonden leaves from Barsta fishing village with a stop in Bönhamn.
tel: +46-613-23005, 42049

## Barsta Fishing Village

See the fisherman's chapel from 1665 and its beautiful ceiling and wall paintings. Accommodations are available by the restaurant Skutskepparn, where you can enjoy a seafood dinner.
tel: +46-613-23090

## Bönhamn Fishing Village

Guest harbour, restaurant, swimming area and 17th century chapel. Accommodations are available.
tel: +46-613-23144, 23127

## Sörleberget

Drive to the top to see the impressive view of the former bays that have been cut off to lakes and the steep cliffs of Ringkalleberget.

## Mannaminne in Häggvik

The artist Anders Åberg has created this museum that focuses on coastal life, art, farming, fishing, emigration, technology, and handcrafts. There is an assortment of buildings - Hungarian and Norwegian houses, a stave church, a café and a restaurant and exhibit facilities.
tel: +46-613-20290

## Norrfällsviken Fishing Village

The picturesque fishing village of Norrfällsviken is located at the outer tip of Mjällom peninsula. The village has a camping grounds and cottages for hire, a swimming area, restaurants, an 18-hole golf course, a guest harbour, and a 225-hectare nature reserve which is primarily made up of shingle fields.
Camping - tel: +46-613-213 82
fax: +46-613-21007

*The climbing trail on Skuleberget Mountain*
*Slåttdalsskrevan Crevice*
*The High Coast Hiking Trail*

# Additional reading

Ahl M, Andersson U B, Lundqvist T and Sundblad K, *Rapakivi granites and related rocks in central Sweden*, 1997, Sveriges geologiska undersökning CA 87.

Bergsten F, *The land uplift in Sweden from evidence of the old water marks*, 1955, Geografiska annaler, volume 36.

Cato I, *On the definitive connection of the Swedish time scale with the present*, 1987, Sveriges geologiska undersökning CA 68.

Ekman K, *The Forest of Hours*, 1999, Vintage.

Ekman M, *A consistent map of the postglacial uplift of Fennoscandia*, 1996, Terra Nova 8.

Fredén C, *The Quaternary history of the Baltic. The western part. I V. Gudelis & L.-K. Königsson, The Quaternary history of the Baltic*, 1979, Acta Universitas Upsalaensis Annum Quingentesimum Celebrantis 1.

Fredén C (editor), *National Atlas of Sweden*, 1994, Geology.

Koistinen T, Stephens M B, Bogatchev V, Nordguten Ö, Wennerström M. and Korhonen J, *Geological map of the Fennoscandian shield*, Geological surveys of Finland, Norway and Sweden, and the North-West Department of Natural Resources of Russia, 2001.

Lundqvist J, Beskrivning till jordartskarta över Västernorrlands län och förutvarande Fjällsjö kommun. *English summary: Description for the map of Quaternary deposits in the county of Västernorrland with northern Ångermanland. Map scale 1:200,000*, 1987, Sveriges geologiska undersökning CA 55.

Lundqvist T, Gee D, Kumpulainen R, Karis L, Kresten P, Beskrivning till Berggrundskartan över Västernorrlands län. *English summary: Bedrock geology of Västernorrland County. Maps in scale 1:200 000*, 1990, Sveriges geologiska undersökning BA 31.

Mascher Jan W, *The Flora of Ångermanland*, 1990, Svensk botanisk tidskrift.

Nordlund C, Det upphöjda landet: Vetenskapen, landhöjningsfrågan och kartläggningen av Sveriges förflutna, 1860-1930. *English summary: The Elevated Land: Science, Land Elevation and the Formulation of a Swedish Past, 1860-1930*, 2002, Kungliga Skytteanska Samfundet.

Sjöberg B (editor), *Sea and coast. National Atlas of Sweden*, 1992.

The County Administration of Västernorrland:
1999 - *The High Coast, 5 000 years of human history*, Högberg L.
2000 - *The High Coast World Heritage Area, formed by 10 000 years of land uplift*, Högberg L.
2000 - The High Coast, enclosure 1: *Glacio-isostatic uplift, a global view*, Fredén C.
2000 - The High Coast, enclosure 3: *Life in the sea*, Bader P.
2000 - The High Coast, enclosure 4: *Cultural landscape and history*, von Stedingk H.
2000 - The High Coast, enclosure 7: *Vegetation and land uplift in the High Coast*, Mascher J W.
2000-2003 - Brochures about the High Coast area and places to visit.

*The High Coast Trail*, 2001, Kramfors and Örnsköldsvik municipalities.

*The Nature Guide of Örnsköldsvik, Sweden*, 2000, Örnsköldsvik municipality.

*World Heritage Sites in Sweden*, 2002, The National Heritage Board.

# Photo credits

**Margareta Bergvall** (46:2, 69:3)
**Lars-G Candell** (25:1, 26, 36, 40:5, 43, 43:3, 51:2, 62:3, 64:2, 68:3, 68:4)
**John Chang McCurdy** (6, 7)
**Per-Olof Engdahl** (50:1)
**Anita Forssell** (16:1, 16:2, 46:1)
**Curt Fredén** (38:1)
**Lars Guvå** (34, 52:1, 52:2, 58:1)
**Britt-Mari Lindström** (9:2)
**Kjell Ljungström** (8:1, 10, 11, 14, 15, 22, 23, 24:2, 29, 31, 39:1, 40, 41, 40:1, 40:3, 42:2, 44, 45, 56, 57:1, 57:2, 59:4, 60, 61, 62:1, 63:3, 63:4, 64:3, 66, 67, 68, 69, 69:1, 70, 72:1, 72:2)
**Bengt A Lundberg** (49, 55)
**Jan A G Lundqvist** (24:1, 43:1, 43:2, 48)
**Rolf Löfgren** (39:2)
**Lennart Mehle** (68:2, 69:2)
**Jan W Mascher** (13, 20, 38:2, 41:1, 41:2, 41:4, 41:5, 58:3, 59:2, 63:1)

**Maria Schibbye** (33, 35, 37)
**Lennart Vessberg** (12, 40:2, 40:4, 41:3, 42:1, 58:2, 58:4, 59:3, 62:2)
**Anders Viotti** (9:1, 68:1)
**Metria** (8:2, 25:2, 59:1, 63:2, 64:1)
Aerial photographs approved for distribution: Skuleberget 992282058-11, Nora 992282015-12, Trysunda 992284026-09, Norrfällsviken 992282024-03, Högbonden 992282017-18. National Land Survey of Sweden 23-05-2002.

# Illustrations

**Lars Högberg**
**Eva Nordqvist** (maps)

A special thanks to Carina Ljungström for providing photographs taken by her husband Kjell Ljungström, who died in Febraury 2000 at the age of 43 before realising his dream of producing a book of photographs on the High Coast.